The Human Knowledge of Christ

The Human Knowledge of Christ

The Knowledge, Fore-knowledge and Consciousness, Even in the Pre-paschal Period, of Christ the Redeemer

BY BERTRAND DE MARGERIE, S.J.

St. Paul Editions

NIHIL OBSTAT:
   Rev. Richard V. Lawlor, S.J.
   Censor Deputatus

IMPRIMATUR:
   + Humberto Cardinal Medeiros
   Archbishop of Boston

Library of Congress Cataloging in Publication Data

Margerie, Bertrand de
   The Human Knowledge of Christ

1. Jesus Christ—Knowledge and learning.
I. Title.
BT590.K6M37   232   80-24456

ISBN 0-8198-3301-0
ISBN 0-8198-3302-9 (pbk.)

Reprinted with permission from *Esprit et Vie,*
June 30, 1977.

Printed in the U.S.A. by the Daughters of St. Paul
50 St. Paul's Ave., Boston, MA 02130

The Daughters of St. Paul are an international congrega-
tion of religious women serving the Church with the com-
munications media.

Contents

SUMMARY

1. Classical Christology teaches, and the Magisterium also, that, long before Easter, Jesus enjoyed in His human intelligence a three-fold knowledge: acquired, infused and beatific. The first kind came to Him, as it does to other men, from the exercise of His senses and His reason; the second was immediately communicated to His human soul by His Divine Person, and the third gave Him immediate knowledge of His Father.

2. This classical Christology is anxious to emphasize not only what Jesus knew as a man, but further and above all that He knew all that was necessary for the perfect carrying out of His mission as Savior and Redeemer.[1] It is as a man that Jesus is Priest and carries out the sacrifice of our Redemption; i.e., He can expiate humanly only what He knows humanly. All the problems relative to the human knowledge of Jesus, classical theology places within the global vision of His mission as the new Adam, repairer of original sin and of all the faults resulting from it.

3. Today, this doctrine is often denied and rarely affirmed. Many exegetes and famous theologians are setting it aside in various ways. What are their principal arguments and how can they be answered?

4. It seems that the three principal objections to the traditional teaching of the Church concerning the three-fold human knowledge of Jesus Christ are: a) it is alleged to have no basis in the New Testament; b) it seems to imply a negation of the humanity of Jesus; c) lastly, it is said to involve an inner contradiction.

Let us take up these points in succession and show how these accusations lack consistency.

Is the Doctrine of the Triple Human Knowledge of Jesus Really Without Support in the New Testament?

5. The evolution of the presentation of the texts of the New Testament concerning the human knowledge of Jesus can be summed up as follows[2]: it has departed from a Christology from above, the Johannine type, to a Christology of a Markan

type, which they consider from below. Formerly it began by emphasizing what Jesus knew in the light of St. John's gospel (2:25; 3:32; 16:30); afterwards it explained in this light the Synoptics (Lk. 2:52; Mk. 13:32) which, at first sight, indicate both the progress and the limits of this knowing. Today many authors proceed in an opposite direction. They start with the analysis of the gospel data concerning the apparent limits, and subsequently find themselves embarrassed by the Johannine texts, and by those of the often overlooked Magisterium.[3]

6. The supposition underlying this method is a certain mistrust with respect to the historicity of John's gospel, in spite of all the works which have demonstrated its credibility and insisted on its accuracy as regards dates and places.[4]

7. Even while admitting, with Lagrange and many others, the particular tone given to the facts by the author of the Fourth Gospel and to the discourses which are reported, we think ourselves in no way bound to cease relying on him in order to know better—in harmony with the very finality he pursued as he wanted to complete the Synoptics—the Jesus of history

and the fullness of His human knowledge. We profess together with the Church of all times and with that of Vatican II[5] the historicity of the gospels, not only of the Synoptics but also of the Gospel which Origen qualified as *spiritual* and which was written expressly to affirm against the Docetists, the reality of the *flesh* assumed by the Word.

8. After recalling these necessary methodological points, we do not intend to justify the acquired knowledge of the Savior—which no one contests today, unlike what occurred in early Christianity and even in the Middle Ages. It will be sufficient (in order to reply to the objections mentioned) to show the New Testament foundation for the teaching of the Church on the infused knowledge and the beatific vision of Christ the Redeemer.

Infused Knowledge

9. a) It is above all *infused knowledge* which seems to be denied by a number of theologians and by certain exegetes, either explicitly or implicitly. K. Rahner, for instance, exalts the immediate vision by Jesus of the divine essence, but minimizes infused knowledge. Malevez answers him very aptly:

According to the gospel accounts, Jesus announced that wherever the good news would be proclaimed in the whole world, the memory of his anointing by a woman in the house of Simon the Leper would be preserved (Mk. 14:9); he predicted Peter's denial; he promised after his death to send the Holy Spirit (Jn. 15:26). Unless one wishes to renounce the authenticity of these words and other similar sayings, one must admit the presence in Jesus of specific knowledge of the future, in the form of objective and thematic representations. How could they be formed in his human consciousness? According to Rahner, one would have to say that these representations relative to the future, like all the others, appeared because of the thematization, the interpretation which was required by the fundamental decision of Jesus reacting to the world around him. But that is precisely what can scarcely be understood: the encounter with empirical reality does not give a sufficient principle of explanation for acquiring objective knowledge concerning the future. It is difficult to include here the economy of an infused knowledge, and we mean the infused objective knowledge which can be conceived of as the fruit of an actualization from pre-reflective knowledge brought about directly by the Spirit of Jesus (directly and not mediated by the world around him). Which amounts to saying that Jesus possesses, besides immediate vision and besides "acquired knowledge" ...an objective infused knowledge of everything "that God wants him to know in order to fulfill his mission."[6] his mission."[6]

10. One could not deny the infused knowledge of Christ[7] without denying also His prophetic mission, constantly affirmed by the New Testament. It could be denied only by rejecting completely the historicity of John's gospel which insists upon this on numerous occasions, in the presence of the disciples, the Samaritan woman, Judas, the Twelve (2:19-25; 4:17-18; 6:66, 64, 70; 11:11). But John makes a careful distinction between the prophetic knowledge of Jesus, and either His knowledge in the vision of the Father (6:46) or His acquired knowledge; Jesus learned; He has heard (9:35) that the Pharisees had expelled the man born blind, while He knows, since the beginning, those who do or do not believe in Him and he who will hand Him over and He sees Nathanael on the one hand, His Father on the other (1:48; 6:46).

11. It must even be said: the Christ of John's gospel is no less a prophet than a

thaumaturge, and it is above all by ascertaining that Jesus knows everything (16:30) that the disciples arrive at the affirmation, temporary only, of their faith in Him. But the conscious and deliberate distinction that John establishes between what Jesus knows and sees, on the one hand, what He understands on the other, shows clearly his intention of affirming, á propos of particular and concrete cases such as that of Judas, knowledge that Jesus had which did not come from experience: the knowledge of the Prophet.

12. The Johannine insistence on the knowledge of Christ as prophet is in perfect harmony with the Old Testament information about the ancient prophets. As R. Otto and A. Feuillet[8] have brought out, one cannot refuse to Jesus

> the charism of foreseeing the future, a privilege which the great prophets had already possessed in the Old Testament and which we find again in the New Testament, for example in the case of Agabus who tells Paul about his coming captivity (Acts 21:10, 11) and in the case of the Apostle of the Gentiles himself (Acts 21:22; 27:22) warned by the Holy Spirit that chains and persecution awaited him and who at the time of his shipwreck on the way to Rome

declares to the passengers that none of them will perish. But foreseeing the future does not imply necessarily total light on that future. Paul at the same time knows and does not know what awaits him (Acts 20:22).

13. Not only would certain people be disposed to say the same about Jesus and to imagine a Christ who was partially ignorant of His own future, but more than one contemporary exegete seems to concede that Christ might be mistaken in His foreseeing and His teaching about the future. Thus it is that an Oscar Cullmann[9] "attributes to Jesus not only ignorance as to the time of the end, but He very positively announces a short delay" in His eschatological discourses.

This view, which others are spreading also, seems to us to have contributed most in recent years to the weakening of faith among a certain number of our priests and seminarians. As Fr. Malevez observed in 1967, this opinion ascribes to Jesus "a considerable error" and "its gravity would be such as to justify among Christians the gravest doubts about the person of Jesus and about His claim to be the supreme divine messenger," since Jesus, by preceding with an Amen His assertion of the precise proximity, for the present generation, of the *absolutely* final event, is said to have covered this error with all His authority.[10]

> In the eyes of the believer, a principle which involves such threatening consequences for his faith can only be fallacious: it cannot be that Jesus has placed all his power in the erroneous affirmation of a proximate end.[11]

Similarly J. Jeremias thinks that the prophecies of Jesus have not been realized and what he says in various places would logically lead to the conclusion that Jesus was a false prophet.[12]

14. What we have just indicated shows that what is at stake today is not only the reality of the infused and prophetic knowledge of Christ, but even His veracity. Obviously, if certain people hesitate to recognize Jesus as a prophet, others are reluctant to see in Him a prophet of truth.

15. Here again Fr. Malevez has reminded us, after Fr. Calès and many others, that

> The eye of seers takes in with one glance successive events, some of which must serve as preludes and preparation for others, in type or in symbol.... In a given description it is often difficult to distinguish the features which belong to figurative phases from the figured phases.[13]

If Jesus really said, as must be admitted, that the end is near (Mk. 13:30, Lk. 21:32) it concerns the end present in figure, the end of a world (with the fall of Jerusalem), symbolizing with singular force the end of the world in such a way as to make it real.[14]

Knowledge of Vision

16. b) If Christ is a prophet never in error, it is precisely[15] because He enjoys as man the vision of the Father, a vision which is "the supreme source of infallibility and immutability in the perception of truth"[16] by the human soul of the Man-God.

Christ Himself tells us that His teaching is worthy of belief because He speaks of what He has seen. "We speak of what we know and we attest to what we have seen.... He who comes down from heaven witnesses to what he has seen and heard, but his testimony none accept. But I say what I have seen with my Father" (Jn. 3:11, 31-32, 8:38). The Gospel of John specifically presents Christ as superior to Moses for that reason: Moses has not seen God (cf. Jn. 1:18 "no man has ever seen God") while Jesus has seen and continuously sees the Father who, in this context draws men to His Son as an infallible Master: "Whoever hears and

learns from the Father comes to me. No
one has seen the Father except he who
comes from God; he it is who has seen the
Father" (Jn. 6:45-46).

It is precisely to guarantee the truth
and credibility of His teaching and His person that Jesus presents Himself as the
Seer of the Father. In 6:46, John uses the
verb in the perfect tense ("eŏraka") emphasizing the lasting result of the action of
seeing. Jesus is always the seer of the
Father.[17]

Human Vision

17. But the teaching that Jesus bases on
such seeing is not given to the Word,
separate from His humanity, but to the
Word made flesh (Jn. 1:14). The teaching
which He receives from the Father (Jn.
7:16), He transmits with a human voice,
not without having understood it with His
human intelligence. As Billot has pointed
out, Jesus did not teach like a gramo-
phone which teaches a foreign language,
but by humanly understanding the meaning and import of the teaching which He
hands on in His own language after having received it from the Father. To claim
that Jesus did not as man understand
what He was preaching would be to fall
into Docetism, would deny the reality of

His humanity and would be contrary to the "sensus fidelium" as well as the constant mind of the Church.[18]

It is then from a *human* vision of the Father that Christ draws His infused knowledge of the teaching which He has the mission of transmitting to the world as the Revealer, and as the ultimate Revealer, superior to Moses. When He asserts that this vision is the source of His credibility as Teacher, it is not a question primarily and above all of a vision that belongs to Him as Word existing before Moses and Abraham, but of a vision which is His as the Word made flesh, as a man teaching men in a human way. It is because He sees, as Man, His Father, that Jesus knows what is in man and can express in concepts and language intelligible for all generations to come the secrets of the Father.[19] As F. M. Braun says, "the Johannine Christ always expresses Himself as the Incarnate Word, at the same time as God and as man,"[20] which could not always be said of all the acts of Christ.[21]

18. Christ, seer of the Father: this affirmation of the Gospel of St. John is indirectly confirmed by a fact already noted more than once. John never calls *faith* the knowledge that Christ had of God. If one

recalls that John speaks 98 times in his Gospel about faith, one will realize that this is a conscious omission, which is equivalent to an exclusion.

The Johannine Christ is the true branch, the true vine faithful to the Father and who trusts Him[22] to the degree of asking Him to save Him (15:1; 12:27); but He is not a believer because He sees His Father. One could even say paradoxically that Jesus is the divine and sublime unbeliever! He does not transmit a message in which He first had to believe: He testifies to what He sees. He does not blindly adhere to the word of the Father; He is Himself the Word equal to the Father.[23]

19. The testimony of the Gospel of John matches here that of the Synoptics: "no one knows the Father except the Son, and he to whom the Son wishes to reveal himself" (Mt. 11:27). A. Vogtle comments on this declaration of Jesus as follows:

> This solemn affirmation contains the idea that his unique authority as a revealer is rooted in the extraordinary and immediate knowledge of God which he possesses as Son.[24]

One must add here the considerations presented above: it is not only as Son, but also as man that Jesus speaks, in a human language, to men about what He learns directly from the Father. There is no mediator between the unique Father and His unique Son, the unique mediator between God and men.

20. Many contemporary exegetes and theologians recognize that there is a solid basis in the New Testament for the triple human knowledge of Jesus, our Redeemer. The real situation is different from the impression that a hasty reader of modern works might conclude. Let us not forget that the truth of the doctrines of the Church never depends on the consent of the theologians and exegetes. It results from the special charism given to the Magisterium by the Holy Spirit. Its denial in the case at hand ends up in a kind of Docetism (that is a reduction to mere appearance) of the revealing function of Jesus as presented in the New Testament. Is it not likely that such teaching is of itself the fruit of Docetism?

Can Such Teaching Be Compatible with the Authenticity of Christ's Human Nature?

21. The conviction of its incompatibility is behind much of the exegetical and theological writing of late. We are told:

> The maintaining of fixed zones of consciousness in Christ involves implicitly the denial of unity in his consciousness.[25]

The accusations brought against classical Christology are summed up in a word: it offers an *artificial* solution. The expression is constantly repeated. They aver that the classical teaching presents an artificial Christ, a Christ who pretends to be ignorant when He is not, who pretends not to know what He really knows, a Christ with mental reservations. The classical doctrine would be mistaken about an important point: human nature cannot be real without ignorance from the beginning and without progress in knowing. This doctrine would be infected with an incurable "neo-docetism."

22. We find that this tendency gives evidence of a very superficial acquaintance with a whole series of nuanced statements among the reflections of

classical theologians on this subject, as well as the more recent contributions.

First of all, by affirming the acquired and experimental knowledge of Jesus, Catholic theology has never ceased admitting that at this level Jesus really passed from ignorance to knowledge. This acquired knowledge experienced increase and progress; in this respect classical theologians are not embarrassed by Saint Luke's words (2:52), "Jesus grew in wisdom before God and men." Jesus, in this way, is the model for all Christians, for all men, since according to the divine plan, all men are ideally called to incorporation in Christ.

23. Moreover, modern psychology, by emphasizing the distinction between the unconscious, the sub-conscious and psychological consciousness, has prepared us to admit the possibility of a real affective plurality in a single consciousness. In this way J. Maritain suggests the existence in Christ of a "supra-consciousness, of the mind divinized by the beatific vision." He refers to "solar consciousness" as opposed to "twilight consciousness" which is possessed in common by Christ and all other viators. In contrast with the latter, the former is a "total unconscious" without the possibility of the man Jesus ex-

pressing in concepts the content of the vision to the evidence of which infused knowledge participated. This divinized supra-consciousness was the heaven of the soul of Christ, as opposed to the twilight of His here below.[26]

Concerning the Day of Judgment

24. Let us take the most difficult case: the exegesis of Mark 13:32: "But of that day or that hour no one knows, not even the angels in heaven, nor the Son, but only the Father."

For many modern exegetes and theologians, it would amount to a pure and simple avowal of ignorance on the part of the Son, as to the day of judgment. A. Vogtle goes so far as to speak of a "fact that is scarcely contestable."

> If the words of Mk. 13:32 were pronounced by Jesus in the form we know, he affirmed that he did not know the time of the eschatological revelation, and this *in as much as* he is Son.[27] (The emphasis is ours.)

However this author seems to con-tradict himself on the one hand, and on the other not to have carefully estimated the scope of his statement. In the same study[28] he speaks also of the "extraordinary and immediate knowledge of God that Jesus possesses *as Son*" (the emphasis is ours); but as Son, Jesus possesses a divine knowledge; it is therefore infinite, it is the same as that of the Father, since the knowledge belongs to their common divine nature. How then could He be ignorant about the day of judgment as Son?

But the error and contradiction of Vogtle are valuable if they oblige us to face the fact that it is impossible to maintain that the Son does not know the hour of judgment precisely as Son, and if He insists that He does not know it, He can be ignorant of it only as man, even while knowing it exactly as Son, as God.

25. In this regard classical theology could and has presented various interpretations.

a) A first solution would be to say: Jesus did not know the hour, either on the level of His experiential knowledge, or on the level of His prophetic and infused knowledge; He knew it only on the level of and by virtue of His human knowledge of the vision of the Father, a knowledge incommunicable in human concepts. As man and even as a prophet Jesus could

say: the Son does not know the hour,
however as seer of the Father and as the
only Son He did know.[29]

b) Another solution seems preferable.
Jesus did not know the hour on the level of
His experiential and acquired knowledge,
but He knew it as prophet who did not
have the mission of revealing it to man. If
it is true that what the seer of the divine
essence knows as such cannot be adequately transmitted in human concepts, it
is nonetheless true, as St. Thomas points
out, that the seer can, as a result of his vision of the divine essence, form within
himself similitudes of the objects which he
has seen. The divine, unique and simple
essence is the (supreme) exemplar of all
the multiple and compound realities, and
God who knows without analysis and
without synthesis is not ignorant of our
complex pronouncements.[30]

26. Anticipating in part what we shall say
in our third part, let us speak precisely
with Billot: for all that relates to the
message which the Father entrusted to
Him, Jesus sees in His beatific vision the
relation and proportion between the
human concepts which He uses and the
transcendent realities that these concepts
translate. One can distinguish between
the *knowing of* articulated concepts in vi-

sion and *knowing by* concepts in their abstract articulation. In the beatific vision Christ, without knowing the truths (which He would propose for our acceptance in faith) in a conceptual way and according to verbal articulation,[31] saw at the same time both the spiritual realities in their wholeness which surpasses conceptual formulation and the concepts which He used in order to communicate them, and the harmony between the realities and their idea. The ideas used by Christ in the delivery of His message are invested with a unique guarantee that makes them irreplaceable. Consequently, the dogmas which are based on formulations emanating from Christ Himself are irrevocable.[32]

What Does the Message Include?

27. Let us not prolong these metaphysical considerations and let us emphasize rather what they demonstrate adequately: the seer of the Father, Jesus, could, without communicating His vision to us, translate into human terms what He saw concerning His mission as Savior and Judge. Mark 13:32 is best explained if one reflects with St. Augustine and Saint

Gregory the Great that this mission did not include the revealing of the hour and the day of judgment. Such an affirmation corresponds perfectly with the reply of the Risen Christ to His disciples about when He was going to restore the Kingdom in Israel: "It is not for you to know the times or seasons which the Father has fixed by his own authority" (Acts 1:7). As Karl Adam said in this regard, "the non-knowing of Christ in Mark 13:32 is a non-wanting-to-know" (sein Nichtwisse ist also ein Nichtwissenwollen).[33]

Let us be further precise on this point well treated by Fr. Galtier in *De Incarnatione ac Redemptione* (Paris, 1947 360, p. 284). If there is an obvious fact in the Gospels, it is that Christ refused consistently to do or to say what did not belong to His mission, confided to Him by His Father. In that first coming, He did not come to judge the world (Jn. 12:47). It did not belong to Him to allow His disciples to sit at His right and at His left, unlike what will happen on the day of judgment (Mt. 25:33 et seq.) for "that is for those to whom my Father has destined it" (Mt. 20:23). He speaks only in the measure and to the extent that His Father sends Him: "He who speaks on his own authority seeks his own glory…. The words that I

say to you, I do not speak on my own..."
(Jn. 7:18; 14:10). No declaration of Jesus
in this respect is as decisive, certainly, as
the one which closes, in the Gospel of
Saint John, what is commonly called the
book of signs:

> I have not spoken on my own
> authority, but the Father who sent
> me has himself given me command-
> ment what to say and what to
> speak.... What I say therefore, I say
> as the Father has bidden me" (Jn.
> 12:49-50).

The disciples had often heard these
declarations. It is not arbitrary to think
that they could, consequently, understand
the meaning of what Christ said: "the Son
does not know the hour or the day of judgment" (Mk. 13:32). That simply meant,
"The Son was not sent in order to tell you
the day and the hour of judgment. As it
did not belong to Him either, in His first
coming, to settle who would sit at His right
or at His left in His Kingdom, nor to reveal
the times and the moment which the Father has placed in His power."

We must note, moreover, that for the
human intelligence of Jesus, to know the
day and the hour of the judgment is secondary in comparison with the knowledge
He has of His Father; or the awareness that

He has of being the judge of humanity; that day and that hour concern the history of this world, contingent with regard to Him as Creator. His soul, plunged into the beatific vision, transcends this world and so does His immutable act embracing in the vision of divine Eternity all the hours of our time, which are the secondary objects of this vision, of which the primordial object is the divine Essence itself. Even for His mission as judge, this day, this hour, in comparison with the judgment to be pronounced, are relatively secondary, without for that reason being deprived of some importance.

As Gregory the Great wrote in the year 600, Christ possessed *in* His humanity a knowledge that did not come *from* it. He insisted that if all things were made by the Word, that means also the hour and day of judgment. Objectively to deny that the Son, as Son, knows the hour and the day of judgment, is to deny His omniscient divinity.[34] Faith in the Incarnation is at stake here.

Christ Is Perfect Man

28. Christ is the Son of God made man. Perfect man is not mere man, an "ordinary" man. Jesus, in as much as He is the Son of God, became human intelli-

gence and liberty, and can only be an *extraordinary* man in a very true sense, a superior man among His brethren. He differs[35] in His very humanity from other men. If one readily acknowledges the privileges of His human liberty, which transcends all men in being able to redeem them, in being the created liberty assumed by their Creator, will it be so difficult to acknowledge the privileges which His human intelligence enjoyed?

His human liberty was not blind, but guided by an intelligence, not ordinarily, but extraordinarily illuminated by the Word.[36] The one whose created liberty could before Easter, without praying, multiply the bread in the desert, cure the man born blind, raise the dead, was also in His human intelligence a unique man, extraordinary, transcending the ordinary measure of human knowledge in His humanity, at the same time being authentically man, consubstantial with our humanity. "Full of grace and truth," He knew "what was in the heart of man, without having to be taught like us."

29. In becoming man, the eternal Son assumed—this is the truth hidden in certain patristic assertions[37]—a human nature of which He only gradually surmounted the experiential ignorance, but

He was at once graced with prophetic knowledge and the knowledge of a seer of the divine essence which befitted His redemptive mission. As the Epistle to the Hebrews points out, it was at the moment of His entrance into the world[38] that Christ embraced the perspective of His sacrificial death (Heb. 10:5-9) "in entering the world." All the mortal life of Christ is redemptive: He could not have been in ignorance at any moment of the sins that He was to expiate, and even "wash in His Blood." We have not been saved by an unconscious and unknowing savior.

30. It remains to point out exactly how, without prejudice to the unity of the human consciousness nor to the sincerity of His language, Christ could know as a prophet what He did not know experientially or could hide from men what He knew.

The classical examples are still valid. The doctor, all men bound by professional secrecy, and above all the confessor, know secrets that they have no reason to transmit but, on the contrary, must keep secret, and with regard to these they must also, when questioned, answer (without deceiving anyone) that they know nothing. The unity of their psychological consciousness is not because of this severed. Likewise to know how to keep a secret without having recourse to an untruth, far from being contrary to the authenticity of humanity, far from being an "artifice," demonstrates an authentic development of human nature. The profound unity of the human nature of Christ had and continues to have its supreme source in its divine "I," unifying in the love which He returns to His Father all the tendencies of His human nature and all its knowledge.

Nor is there in the reply of Jesus reported in Mark (13:32) a *"purely* mental reservation"; the disciples could guess perfectly well that the Prophet Jesus was unwilling to reveal what He knew, having no mission to reveal it. Jesus Himself had already said previously to His "brethren" that He would not go up to Jerusalem so as to signify that He would not go up publicly, and this did not prevent Him from "going up secretly, without being seen" (Jn. 7:3-10). Jesus would not have been truly man, if He had not given us the example of a legitimate mental reservation. Moreover the Revealer deliberately limited, held back the fullness of His pre-paschal revelation: "I have still many things to tell you, but you cannot bear them now" (Jn. 16:12).

Even after Easter, the exact words about the day and the hour of judgment, either individual or collective, do not form part of the message that Christ and His Church are to transmit to the world; the famous verse in Mark becomes more intelligible if one links it to the one immediately following: "Watch, for you know not when the hour will be" (Mk. 13:33 *et seq.*).

31. The teaching of the triple *human* knowledge of Jesus does not imply the denial of His humanity, any more than the teaching of the double knowledge, the ordinary and the prophetic, of the prophet, of any prophet (who is not the only Son of God).

If one admits that the prophet is no less man because he is a prophet and that God his Creator does not diminish the reality of his human nature by adding to it the charism of prophecy, one will be equally disposed to recognize that the Word has not suppressed, but crowned the real human nature by actualizing at once a potentiality inherent in all created intelligence: that of vision face to face. The only Son, full of grace and truth, who sees His Father when no one has ever seen God, became flesh and a human word precisely to tell us what He saw in His Father: He is no less flesh for having seen it and said so.[39]

Is It Contradictory To Affirm That a "Viator Enjoys the Beatific Vision"?

32. The objection is: if Jesus saw and knew everything in God, how could He learn anything at all in a human way?

They insist: if Jesus experienced in the face to face vision of His Father a perfect joy, how could He suffer here below?

> How can one affirm that Christ drank to the dregs the chalice of suffering inherent in his dereliction and death, if his soul enjoyed at the same time an unsurpassed celestial joy to the highest degree? It behooves us certainly to examine whether first of all the coexistence of the unspeakable affliction and unspeakable happiness is possible in a human soul.[40]

33. To the first objection the reply[41] is: we have already seen that the scholar and the ordinary man do not know the same reality in the same way. But the scholar does not think nor express himself always like a scholar; he can from time to time make

use of his knowledge or not make use of it; ways of knowing that are perfectly distinct coexist in him without prejudice to each other. The same man can be at the same time an historian, a chemist, and a philosopher, consequently looking at the same object in different ways.

34. To the second objection one must answer: the *human* beatitude of Jesus was *perfect but not complete.* The plenitude of joy (cf. Jn. 15:11; 17:13) results in the possession by the soul of the Supreme Good, but the human will even in this state can direct itself to certain other created objects, conferring on him a joy (or by their absence a privation or a suffering) that is accidental; the soul can desire absent goods while in possession of the supreme Good. If this supreme Good suffices to satisfy the soul, it does not necessarily confer on it all the created good which it desires. The transcendent Creator, while giving Himself, does not suppress creation.[42]

35. Jesus, seer of the Father, precisely because He wanted to die for our salvation, did not allow His beatific vision to flood Him with joy to the point of suppressing the passibility of His flesh and of the inferior powers of His soul.[43] Such an

affirmation is required as the only possible conciliation of the different facts in the Gospel, presenting Jesus, on the one hand, as seer of the Father, and, on the other, as a man who suffers. Perhaps this is suggested by the Epistle to the Hebrews (12:2): "Jesus, who for the joy that was set before him endured the cross, despising the shame."

36. The life of the saints, the mystics and even many mothers of families give evidence of just such coexistence of a very great joy in "the fine point" of the soul, faced with the perfections and the love of God which dwell there, and of a very acute suffering, not only of the body, but of the mind, painfully wounded by insults or by the sins of those extremely dear to them. Is it not in just such a context that Saint Catherine of Siena understood and expressed the coexistence of the beatific vision and of the passion in the soul of Jesus crucified?[44]

As has been exactly noted,[45] *the experience of the mystics* makes us see that a more perfect knowledge when a higher degree of spiritual life has been reached, does not prevent thereafter—unlike the ecstasies of a lesser degree—either the experience of the senses nor even the exercise of reason. (Think of Mary of the Incarnation associating at the same instant contemplation and calculating). Has not Christ, the leader and prince of all mystics, associated much more deeply still the exercise of His acquired knowledge and that of His infused knowledge?[46]

37. They insist further:

> If Jesus does not know that his action reaches the entire universe and saves humanity, he cannot give his life for it, he can only make his death a beautiful act of generosity; inversely, if Jesus sees in advance the future pass before his eyes like a film, then he is no longer in our world, he is beyond time, more exactly he is outside of all reality, because this filmed future exists only in our imagination, incapable of conceiving the future otherwise than as already realized, in other words as past. This is to misunderstand, according to Bergson's words, that "time is invention or it is nothing at all." It is to misunderstand also, according to a false concept of the creative knowledge of God, the dignity of man.[47]

The Fullness of the Knowledge of Christ

38. Here the necessity of recognizing a certain fullness in the knowledge of Christ as

Savior is admitted, then narrowly limited. Ought not one rather recognize that if the immortal soul of every man already dominates his own temporality ("Intelligence is above time," says St. Thomas of Aquinas),[48] Christ, as a man endowed with the charism of prophecy and seer of the Father dominates time still more, to the point of being very truly beyond our time, of transcending our world by one whole side of His human nature such as it exists in the concrete? Did not Jesus say: "You are from below; I am from above; you are of this world, I am not of this world" (Jn. 8:23)?

39. On the other hand, is it exact to say that "time is an invention or nothing at all"? The text cited above misunderstands what the Bible and the Church say about the real existence of a charism of prophecy which presupposes essentially the foreknowledge of future and contingent events.[49] We will not repeat here what we already quoted of Malevez against K. Rahner. Rather we should like to insist that the prophet in his privileged participation in the eternal wisdom of God, *knows future events in their "presentiality."* As J. Maritain says, the eternal plan is not "a scenario planned in advance," since there is no succession for God, since

He does not foresee but sees all things "and in particular the choices and the free decisions of the created existent, which, in as much as they are free, are absolutely unforeseeable." He sees them in the very instant they occur in the pure existential freshness of their emergence into being, in the humility of their own instant birth.[50]

The divine knowledge is creative. The prophet, to be sure, does not participate in this aspect, but how can it be denied that he participates in the manner of knowing a presence which for others is still an absence...?

One cannot see either how "the dignity of man" would be misjudged by the charism of prophecy which exalts this man by emphasizing his participation in the eternity of God.

40. We think then that all attempts past, present and no doubt future, to show the contradictions in the teaching of the Church on the triple knowledge of Jesus will always be useless. But we must still mention in passing the most fruitful efforts of Catholic theologians to bring out the harmony between the three types of knowledge in the one Man-God. These efforts have particularly cast light on the necessity of infused knowledge in view of

a revealing mediatization of the immediate knowledge (vision) of the unique Mediator, Revealer and Redeemer.

41. Without this infused knowledge of Prophet, Jesus could not translate into human terms and concepts the knowledge of Himself and of the whole supernatural economy of the Kingdom, a knowledge received in the vision of the Father. Without infused knowledge, Jesus could not make Himself understood by men. With it He supernaturally knew, but in a manner suited to the knowledge of man, all the mysteries of the supernatural order, "all that concerns our reparation" according to the word of St. Bonaventure.[51]

In more contemporary terms we can say that Christ received a created revelation beyond all categories—the beatific vision—a created "categorical" revelation, namely the infused knowledge which was absolutely necessary for His mission as Revealer: together they constitute the whole of created revelation. (The word revelation is here used in the sense of supernatural knowledge without further specification.)

The beatific vision is the condition which makes Revelation possible; the infused knowledge, together with the acquired knowledge, its means of transmission to men. The conceptual is the objectification of the metaconceptual and, therefore, its inevitably imperfect expression. Christ knew how His message corresponded to the reality of His personal mystery, to the transcendental and irreducible light of His human consciousness of Son and of seer of the divine Essence.[52]

The infused knowledge itself has need of acquired knowledge, taking its origin from the experience and from the language learned by Jesus. The revelation of Christ to humanity was not caused but conditioned by human language.[53]

The three types of human knowledge in Jesus constitute the triple possession and the triple act, distinct by its object, but complementary, of the unique intelligence and human consciousness of Christ, without separation.

The blending of these three types of knowing remains a mystery for us[54] like the mystery of the Incarnation of the Word, with this slight difference that here the mystery is situated within the assumed humanity itself. For we only enjoy one of these three types of human knowledge. Christians endowed with the charism of prophecy could have a better understanding of it in the bosom of faith.

Filial and Messianic Consciousness

42. It is easy to see how many problems related to the human knowledge of the pre-paschal Christ are closely linked to the mystery of *filial and messianic consciousness*, about which we want to say a few words in order to reaffirm its unity.

The beloved Son had an awareness of His community of destiny with men, angels and the whole universe. In the strength of His filial consciousness, Jesus knows Himself as Revelation to the Father in the Spirit and in relation to the angels and the world He divinizes. He is perfectly aware of being at the same time Infinite and finite, in relations with the totality of reality. Let us say rather: Jesus is conscious of making reality a whole[55] in a unique way.

That His human consciousness was fully aware is best shown in the two concepts of the Son of Man and the *"Ego eimi,"* of the "I am" magnificently associated in John 8:28: when you have lifted up the Son of Man, you shall know that I am.... Before Abraham was, I am" (Jn. 8:28; 24:56).

On the one hand, in His *human* consciousness, Jesus asserts that He is the One of whom the *"I"* is identical with Being; His human consciousness expresses the content of His divine consciousness.[56]

On the other hand, in calling Himself the *Son of Man,* Jesus expresses His whole mystery, divine and human, personal and functional; His awareness of His pre-existence, of His Incarnation, of His redemptive death and of His glory to come; all that is before time, all that He accomplished in time, all that awaits Him at the end of time; His heavenly origin, His entrance into a humble humanity, and the death awaiting Him as leader of a holy people and His triumph over everything and everybody. Truly this title expresses best His consciousness of Messiah and Son, for He stresses His possession at the same time of a true human nature and His heavenly origin.[57] With this title, the Christology of the New Testament is at its maximum since the outset.[58]

The assertions by Jesus of His prophetic knowledge and His knowledge from vision get all their meaning and all their importance in the context of the 70 times the title "Son of Man" is used. In His prophetic mission the Son of Man shows that He dominates all human time; descended from heaven, He can say the things of heaven where He always is by His vision of the Father (cf. Jn. 3:13, 11; 6:46).

Conclusions

43. We have just insinuated it: the teaching of the Church on the triple human knowledge of the Son of Man flows directly from the affirmations of Jesus Himself making known His knowledge as prophet as well as His mission as Revealer. As for the knowledge acquired by experience and by reasoning, it flows necessarily from the affirmation of the authenticity of the human nature of Jesus. The Church cannot renounce this doctrine without putting itself in contradiction with the New Testament,[59] the ultimate source that makes known the triple human knowledge of Jesus, without contradicting the testimony of Jesus Himself.

This teaching was brilliantly summed up by St. Bonaventure in his famous expression: Christ enjoys in His human soul a triple knowledge *"a Verbo, in Verbo, de Verbo"* (In III Sent. d. 14, a. 2).

Knowledge *a Verbo:* that is both experiential knowledge and infused knowledge which both have their origin in the Word as creator and illuminator.

Knowledge *in Verbo:* here we have the knowledge of secondary objects of the beatific vision, objects seen in the Word.

Knowledge *de Verbo:* here we have the face to face vision of the divine essence itself which is identical with the eternal Word.

All the human knowledges of the Incarnate Word are thus polarized by the Person of the Word (cf. A Sépinski, O.F.M., *La psychologie du Christ chez Bonaventure*, Paris, 1948, ler partie, ch. II and III).

44. The objections raised against this doctrine send us back to the refutation of the modernist doctrines presented by Saint Pius X in the encyclical *Pascendi* in 1907: as he brought out, the modernist exegesis was conditioned by philosophical presuppositions and not caused by biblical texts.[60]

45. Doubtless it will be said that our study, on the contrary, follows apologetic tendencies to which many today refuse to yield. But we could only answer with Fr. Malevez that the repugnance to *apologetics*

seems to us unjustified. Apologetics is a task that faith assigns to itself and accomplishes ("fides quaerens intellectum"). It refuses to recognize as integral to its content any affirmation that would put it in contradiction to itself. And so, faith in Jesus, the supreme divine messenger, repels by an intrinsic exigency the presence in the consciousness of Jesus of an error which He claims to guarantee by His authority[61] or the presence of an ignorance incompatible with His own affirmations (or with those inspired in the authors of Scripture by His Spirit).

Mission of the Holy Spirit in Jesus

46. In order that its import and meaning in the economy of salvation be better perceived, the Catholic doctrine of the triple human knowledge of the Son of Man must be placed in the context of the invisible mission of the Holy Spirit in Him, in the context of faith in the mystery of Redemption, of the duty of consoling the Redeemer and, lastly, of the constantly renewed celebration of the eucharistic sacrifice of the Church.

47. First of all, it seems to us that, unlike the knowledge of vision and the acquired

knowledge, the infused knowledge of
Jesus is the effect of the invisible mission
of the Holy Spirit in the Messiah from the
first instant of the Incarnation.

> In "the immaculate bosom of
> the Virgin, the Son of God embel-
> lished His soul with the Breath of
> grace and truth; the Holy Spirit
> took delight in dwelling in the
> soul of the Redeemer as in His be-
> loved temple; He dwells in Christ
> with such plenitude of graces
> that one cannot conceive of any
> greater" (Pius XII, *Mystici Cor-
> poris).*[62]

Thanks to this charism of infused
knowledge, Christ could from the first instant merit for the human race (at a time
when acquired knowledge was lacking, it
must also be recalled that the beatific
vision was not the principle of merit).

48. By infused knowledge,[63] as by the
knowledge of vision, one can also explain
in Jesus the consciousness of the divine
filiation; the human awareness of this
divine filiation can have no other beginning[64] in Jesus except that of His earthly
existence: "no one had to tell Him who He

was,"[65] the Belgian bishops wrote in 1967. Jesus never had to "search for His identity." In that sense there is no history of the consciousness of Jesus Christ.

49. Next we can and we must say with the Church[66] that at the Last Supper, during His Agony, on the Cross as well as already in the Manger, Jesus knew and loved humanly every human person: "The Son of God loved me and delivered himself up for me" (Gal. 2:20).[67] Otherwise how would He have humanly expiated my sins? How would He have humanly redeemed humanity? His *kenosis* did not consist in the (impossible) suppression of His divine consciousness, nor in the suspension of His human knowledge, but in the painful assumption of the human knowledge of the sins and sorrows of men.[68]

He loved me not only in "His divine form and condition," but in "His form and condition of slave," in His "human form." He loved me in spite of my sins, in order to save me from them and it is because He knew me—and knew them—in that human form that He offered Himself for me.

The Church has never believed that the Man Jesus knew me on the Cross only as God, loved me on the Cross only with a divine love. Never has she believed that the man Jesus as man did not know my sins and my person at the moment when He was dying for my salvation.

50. The *neo-agnoetism*[69] *of the present time* is at least indirectly contrary to the Christian faith in Christ the Redeemer. Unfaithful to Revelation, to the teaching of the Church and to theological reason, it saps piety and deprives the faithful of the consolation of consoling the agonizing Christ, by plunging them into the sad scepticism of Magdalen after the Passion: "They have taken away my Lord and I do not know where they have laid him" (Jn. 20:13).

On the contrary, manifesting how the doctrine of the Church on the triple human knowledge of the Son of Man belongs substantially to Revelation favors that exercise of pure love so dear to Charles de Foucauld,[70] which is called: consoling reparation to the Heart of Jesus, especially in the form of the way of the cross.

Consoling Jesus

51. The classical objection is well known: how could we today console Christ, now perfectly happy and glorious, in His Passion now forever past? Pius XI already in

1928 gave the decisive answer: if we cannot console Him, we cannot offend Him either; if we could offend Him by our sins, and by our present sins, we can also today console Him and affect Him, our Creator, by the good works undertaken with the inspiration of His Spirit. We have, therefore, *the duty to comfort the suffering Christ,* since we are able to do so.[71]

52. Similarly, we can and must *contribute to the human and accidental beatitude of the one who is the blessed God made man.*[72] The astonishing privilege of human persons is to be able to act, so as to make Him suffer or for His beatitude, upon the human heart of a divine Person.

53. Nothing of all that is difficult to grasp on the background of the triple human knowledge of the Son of Man. But its denial, contrary to some particular truths, also endangers the whole of Christian faith. Those who deny either the beatific vision or the pre-paschal Christ, or His infused knowledge as prophet, or both, and claim to take into account the gospel statement in support of divine knowledge and the acquired experiential knowledge of Christ alone, end up their intellectual journey in many cases in agnosticism or even atheism.

54. In any case, we must stress the fact that *the exercise at present of this triple human knowledge of the man Jesus continues in celestial glory and in the mystery of the Eucharist.*

Neither glory nor grace destroys human nature. The heavenly and eucharistic Christ always sees His Father face to face. He continues to exercise infused knowledge unceasingly received from His Spirit and the knowledge already acquired by the senses or by rational reflection.

55. Drawing upon the Thomistic doctrine we can even say that the unique act of the beatific vision perdures unique since the conception of Jesus in the womb of the Virgin, always the same in the dereliction of the Cross, as in the glory of the Resurrection.

The death of Christ is the best phenomenological expression of the immanent action of the beatific vision, accompanied by beatifying love, as we described it in *Christ for the World*.[73] The decision of sacrificial death flows from the love which accompanies the beatific vision: "as I know the Father, I give my life for my sheep" (Jn. 10:15).

56. At the Last Supper while instituting the Eucharist, Christ was at once Priest

and Prophet. It is in order to associate men forever, all men, with the vision of His Father in Himself that the Seer of the Father instituted the Sacrifice and the Sacrament of the new Law. The Eucharist is the principal means by which the saved Savior (Jn. 4:42; 12:27) already as Savior, seeing His Father, wishes to make others partakers of His vision,[74] and so to save them. Does not this institution show in Him an extraordinary infused knowledge of the future of the world and of the Church, until His return?

Jesus and the Communicant

57. When we receive communion we receive the Seer of the Father, the one who sees face to face, who comes to increase our faith by His Spirit, to make us thereby forevermore participants, in it, of the vision towards which He leads us, after having spoken of it and in it. The Wisdom of God made flesh (1 Cor. 1:24), Christ has received, with the Spirit without measure (Jn. 3:34), in this vision, all the treasures of wisdom and knowledge.[75] He in whom the fullness of divinity dwells corporally gives Himself to us sacramentally in order to associate us with His own plenitude (cf. Col. 2:3, 9). He gives us His "higher

reason"[76] contemplating His own eternity and His "knowledge from on high" which becomes in a certain way ours. He wants to make us taste that "very loving intimacy"[77] which He has with each of us since He was in the womb of Mary, in the manger and on the cross. How well He knows and loves us humanly since the beginning, even better and more than each one of us knows and loves himself.

By receiving the Blessed Son, beatified from the first moment of His earthly existence and created in the vision of His own infinite and uncreated Beatitude, we understand better under the influence of His Spirit, to what degree it would have been impossible not to be beatified by such a vision, even if it did not still flow back on His body. The immediate vision of the divine Beatitude can only be beatifying. The Inhumanation of the Word is the beatification of the assumed humanity.[78]

58. The neo-agnoetist errors of our time, often mutually contradictory,[79] will pass like so many others. For all time Christ is Truth. He is the same yesterday and today; He will be so eternally (Hb. 13:8).

59. By giving Himself in Communion, the Eucharistic Heart of Jesus continues to

spur theologians to study the old and new problems[80] relating to His human knowledge and the bishops to present to the faithful this triple knowing. Does not their episcopal magisterium, their charism depend on His vision, on His pre-paschal prophecies and on His earthly teaching which enlightens them always?

Footnotes

1. Here are a few expositions of this Christology: C. Chopin, P.S.S., *Le Verbe Incarné et Rédempleur*, Tournai, 1963, pp. 93-102; B. Leeming, *Adnotationes de Verbo Incarnato*, Rome, 1936, pp. 319-372; R. Garrigou-Lagrange, *De Christo Salvatore*, Rome, 1976, pp. 249-284 (Engl. tr. St. Louis); B. M. Xiberta, *Tractatus De Verbo Incarnato*, Madrid, 1954, pp. 400-412 and 428-430.

Let us recall also the principal documents of the Magisterium of the Church on this subject: the letter *"Sicut aqua"* of Pope St. Gregory the Great to Saint Eulogius, patriarch of Alexandria, in 600 on agnoetism (D.S. 474-476); the propositions 32 to 35 of the decree *Lamentabili* (1907, D.S. 3432-3435); the decree of the Holy Office, in 1918 on the knowledge of Christ (D.S. 3645-3647); the encyclical *Mystici Corporis* of Pius XII, in 1943 (D.S. 3812); and the encyclical *Haurietis aquas* in 1956 (D.S. 3924). This last document is the only one to mention explicitly the infused knowledge of Christ as distinct from His beatific vision. As the encyclical *Haurietis aquas* had not only a parenetic intention, but still was explicitly doctrinal (is it not, besides, the most profound and most complete official treatise on the mystery of Christ by the magisterium of the Church, since the great Christological councils of Chalcedon, Constantinople III and Trent until that of Vatican II?), we can legitimately speak of a doctrine of the Church concerning the triple knowledge of Christ; even if the magisterium did not specifically speak of the "acquired knowledge," this doctrine of the three types of human knowledge in the Man Jesus has been constantly taught by all the theological schools for more than 7 centuries. Although the Church does not present infused knowledge and acquired knowledge as revealed truths, she does not deny that they are, and our work tries to show why they must be affirmed as such.

2. Cf. F.E. Crowe, S.J., *The Mind of Jesus*, in "Communio" (American ed.) 1. (1974) p. 366.

3. As for example A. Vogtle mentions very vaguely the teaching of the Church in explaining Mk. 13:32: *Le message de Jésus et l'interprétation moderne,* Paris, 1969, pp. 41-43. On the point that concerns us, few Catholic exegetes seem preoccupied in reading the Scriptures with and in the Church.

4. Cf. (among others) the new *Bible de Jerusalem,* Paris, 1973, pp. 1525-1526, which sums up perfectly the present state of the question. Let us note that one could establish also the triple human knowledge of the Savior from the Synoptics: Mt. 26:34 (prophecy of the denial of Peter) gives testimony of the infused knowledge of Jesus and Mt. 11:27 for His immediate vision of the Father, by His human soul.

5. Cf. The Dogmatic Constitution on Divine Revelation, *"Dei Verbum,"* nos. 18 and 19, where the Council, after having emphasized the apostolic origin of the four Gospels, proclaims: "The Church affirms without hesitation the historicity of the four Gospels." Some speak today of a post-paschal consciousness of the Evangelists and their rereading after Easter of pre-paschal events; they say also that there may have been several successive layers in the Johannine gospel; all this did not prevent the Evangelists, according to the assertion of the Council *(ibid.),* from "transmitting" in all reality what "the Lord had said and done" before Easter "so as to give us things that were still true and sincere about Jesus." And in the case of John, "based on

their own memory and souvenirs" (ibid.). To present the prophecies of Jesus during His mortal life or His sayings about His immediate knowledge and His vision of the Father as interpretations or adaptations elaborated by the Evangelists without historical foundation would certainly be contrary to the teaching of the Church on the historicity of the Gospels. See also the proposition condemned by the Church in the decree Lamentabili especially á propos of the Gospel of John, D.S. 3414-3418.

6. L. Malevez, S.J., Le Christ et la foi, in Nouv. Rev. Theol. 88 (1966), 1027-1028; cf. K. Rahner, S.J., Dogmatische Erwägungen über das Wissen und Selbstebewusstsein Christi, in Schriften zur Theologie, V (1962), 222-245.

7. Like the majority of theologians, we understand by infused knowledge a knowledge independent in its origin of human experience and yet mediate, conceptual and consequently distinct from immediate knowledge, from beatific vision. The immense majority of theologians today still affirm, I believe, along with C. Duquoc, O.P., that "Christ is the Prophet par excellence, the Revealer. Consequently it is of faith, in the technical sense of that expression, that Christ had a quite unique knowledge of the mystery of God and the plan of salvation" (Christologie, Paris, 1968, t. I, p. 167). The Scotist School also affirms the infused knowledge of Christ the Prophet: see C. Frassen, Scotus academiccus, Paris 1676, t. III, tract. I, Disp. II, art. 11, pp. 248-251.

8. Cf. R. Otto, Reich Gottes und Menschensohn, Munich, 1934; English Trans. London, 1951, pp. 357-363; A. Feuillet, Les trois grandes prophéties de la Passion et de la Résurrection, des Evangiles synoptiques, in Revue Thomiste 67 (1967), 545-546.

9. L. Malevez, *Le Message de Jésus et l'histoire du salut,* in Nouv. Rev. Théol. 89 (1967), 129-131; The author alludes to the work of O. Cullmann *Le salut dans l'histoire,* Meuchâtel, 1966, especially pp. 211-234; he points out the felicitous reaction of Cullmann against Bultmann in favor of the messianic consciousness of Jesus.

10. Malevez. *op. cit., ibid.*

11. Malevez, *ibid.*

12. J. Jeremias, *Théologie du N.T.,* Paris, 1973, especially par. 13 and p. 355. The same author seems to keep complete silence, however, about the *divine* person of Jesus.

13. J. Calès, *Recherches de Science Religieuse,* 11 (1921), 368-369; Malevez, *op. cit.* (no. 9), p. 132.

14. *Ibid.,* p. 133.

15. This is not the immediate reason (in itself infused knowledge would suffice to guarantee this infallibility) but it is the supreme reason: cf. B. de Margerie, *Christ for the World,* Chicago, 1974, p. 231.

16. *Ibid.*

17. B. Leeming, *Cor Jesus,* Rome, 1959. t. I., pp. 626-634.

18. Cf. B. Leeming, *The Human Knowledge of Christ,* in Irish Theological Quarterly 19 (1952), 239 et seq.; L. Iammarrone, OFM Conv., *"L'Unità psicologica di Cristo secondo S. Bonaventura e il suo valore teologico"* in Misc. Francesc. 74 (1974) 123-160. See also by the same author *"L'io psicologico di D. Scoto,"* De Doctrina J.D. Scoti, Roma, 1968. t. III, pp. 291-316 (Actes due Congrès Scotiste International).

19. Y.M.J. Congar, *Jesus Christ,* Paris, 1966, pp. 64-65: "This supernatural wisdom also permitted him to know man in all the depth necessary

to know that human notions and simple words that he used would be sufficient for and truly inexhaustible of men not only until the end of the world through centuries still to come of experiments and new discoveries, but down to the deepest depths Jesus knows the import and infinite value of his words and his acts as man.''

20. F.M. Braun, O.P., *Jean le Théologien*, t. III, 1: *Le Mystère de J.-C.*, Paris 1966, p. 222; cf. p. 213 St. Augustine had a different view. In Jo. tract. 99, 1 (ML 35. 1886). But perhaps the difference is only in emphasis. One could object with Galtier (*De Incarnatione ac Redemptione*, Paris 1947, par. 329, pp. 258-259), because of the declaration of Christ promising to send the Paraclete (John 15:26): would it not be as Word and not as man that Jesus said that? But St. Thomas observes (*Summa Theol.*, III a, 8, 1, 1) that Christ could as man give the Holy Spirit, since His humanity was the instrument of His divinity. He refers to St. Augustine (who seems not to have recognized this category of instrumental causality) and explains his thought in a satisfying way. The explanation of the Angelic Doctor takes into account the depths of Jn. 20-22: "He breathed on them and said: Receive the Holy Spirit": it is certainly both as Word and as man (instrument of the Word) that Christ was speaking. One can also explain in this way the words of Jesus reported in Jn. 15:26. See *Le Christ pour le Monde*, Paris, 1971, pp. 391-394.

21. The creation and active spiration of the Spirit are acts of the Word and not of the Word incarnate.

22. Cf. L. Malevez, *Le Christ et la foi*, in N.R. Th. 1966 p. 1910, where the author nuances the position of H. Urs von Balthasar in *La foi du Christ*, Paris, 1968.

23. J. Alfaro, S.J., "Encarnación y Revelación," *Gregorianum*, 1968, p. 436-437; N.T. does not present Jesus as a believer but as the faithful Son, object of our own faith.

24. A. Vogtle, *Message de Jésus et interprétation moderne, op. cit.*, p. 108. He could reconsider in the light of the exegesis given here his interpretation of Mk. 13:32 *(ibid.*, p. 43); cf. n. 3; in the same light C. Duquoc could also overcome the curious internal contradiction contained in his *Christologie*, t. I, p. 168, where after having mentioned that the metaphor of the vision implies immediacy (line 16), he lets it be understood that the pre-paschal Christ did not see "God in the immediacy of his essence" (lines 26-27).

25. E. Gutzwenger, S.J., "La science du Christ," *Concilium*, 11 (1965), 83.

26. J. Maritain, *De la grâce et de l'humanité de Jésus*, Bruges, 1967, pp. 52-71; cf. B. de Margerie, S.J., *Science et Esprit*, 20 (1968), 158-159. See also E. Bailleux, "La conscience humaine de Jésus," *Mélanges de Sc. Rel.*, 25 (1968), 37: "The source of consciousness lies in the super-consciousness which St. Augustine calls the memory and certain moderns call the transcendental ego."

27. A. Vogtle, *op. cit.*, p. 43.

28. *Ibid.*, p. 108.

29. As in E. Bailleux, "La plénitude des temps dans le Christ," *Revue Thomiste*, 71, (1971), 14-15, especially in note 29.

30. St. Thomas, *Sum. Theol.*, Ia, 12, 9, 2, (cf. IIa-IIae. 174. 3); and *Summa contra Gentiles*, I.58 sub fine.

31. An allusion to infused knowledge.

32. As quoted by J.J. Latour in his remarkable unpublished thesis, sustained at the Institut Catholique de Parism in 1960: *La vision beatifique du Christ*, t. II, p. 309.

33. Karl Adam, *Der Christus des Glaubens*, Düsseldorf, 1954, p. 297. In order to support his interpretation, he quotes the parallel texts of Mt. 7:22 and 25:13: Lagrange has magnificently extended the exegesis of St. Augustine and St. Gregory the Great in his commentary of the *Evangile selon Saint Marc* (pp. 326-327): "This exegesis may appear too subtle." "It is solid, however, if one takes into account that the term Father means God as the inaccessible and hidden one (Jn. 1:18). He communicates Himself to men by the Son and He communicates with them by the ministry of the angels. That which must absolutely remain secret is not part of the mission of the Son nor of the angels. In as far as one distinguishes the Son from the Father as sent by Him to men, the Son does not have this secret in His attributes." This view will be completed by the profound interpretation of St. Thomas Aquinas: "If one says that the Father knows the day of judgment, it is because He communicates this knowledge to the Son." In other words it is as Father, who gives everything to His Son (Mt. 11:27) that the Father knows the day of judgment. The Angelic Doctor added: "The Son knows the day of judgment not only according to His divine nature, but even according to His human nature. For, as St. John Chrysostom shows (hom 77), if it was given to Christ as man to know how He was to judge, with greater reason must He have known the time of the judgment, which is a less important thing" (IIIa, 10.2.1).

34. S. Grégoire, Letter *Sicut aqua*, DS 475: "Incarnatus Unigenitus factusque pro nobis homo perfectus *in* natura quidem humanitatis novit diem et horam judicii, sed tamen hunc non *ex* natura humanitatis novit."

35. Cf. F.E. Crowe, *lec. cit.*, p. 384: "Jesus is different." One could bring up as an objection Hb. 2:17, 4:15: "Jesus had to become in all things like his brothers...experienced in all things in a similar way except sin." St. Robert Bellarmine interpreted the text correctly: "*In all things* refers to all that belongs to the perfection of nature or to everything that leads to Redemption. Otherwise Christ would not have been conceived of the Holy Spirit, nor born of a Virgin, nor ignorant of the rebellions of the lower side of human nature; He would even have to be afflicted with fevers and other maladies" (Second general controversy on Christ, Bk. IV, ch. 5; *Opera Omnia,* Paris, Vivès, 1870, t.I, p. 405).

36. Pie XII, *Haurietis Aquas,* DS 3924; *Mystici Corporis,* DS 3812.

37. By extension St. Athanasius says: "Christ wanted to carry in His flesh human ignorance in order to redeem it and to purify humanity completely" (MG 26:624); or St. Cyril of Alexandria: "For love of us, He did not refuse to lower Himself to bear our miseries among which is ignorance" (MG 75:369). See J. Lebreton, S.J., "L'ignorance du jour du jugement," *Rech. de Sc. Rel.,* 8 (1918), 281-289; see also A. Michel "Science de Jésus Christ" in DTC 14, a (1914), 1628-1665 especially col. 1640-1647.

38. *Ibid.,* col. 1654 (texte de E. Hugon, *Le mystère de l'Incarnation,* p. 276-277); Vogtle, *op. cit.,* p. 99: no beginning of messianic consciousness.

39. Cf. Jn. 1:14, 18; 8:38. In spite of H. Urs von Balthazar ("the inalienable nobility of man is to be able, to be obliged even, to freely plan his life for a future that he does not know. To deprive Jesus of this chance would amount to depriving Him of His dignity as man," *La foi du Christ,* Paris, 1968, p. 281), ignorance, as St. Augustine has shown, is not a characteristic constitutive of human nature,

but a result of original sin; Christ came precisely as a Redeemer of that fallen nature; it is on this point one can trace a "consensus" of the Fathers in regard to the Christological controversy of the VIth and VIIth centuries (cf. DTC, *doc. cit.*, col. 1646-1647) and of the agnoetists. One cannot help being astonished to see Urs von Balthazar, a great student of the Fathers, not following them in this instance. The Greek Fathers arrived at the same conclusion as St. Augustine by a different path: ignorance is the source of sin and therefore the Redeemer cannot assume it.

40. Gutzwenger, art. cité, (n. 25), p. 82.

41. For example, J.J. Latour, *op. cit.* (n. 32).

42. Fr. Galtier, *De Incarnatione ac Redemptione*, Paris, 1947,§ 445, pp. 350-351, n. 1; A. Koller, S.C.J., *Reparation to the S. Heart, Theology of Consolation*, ed. The Priests of the S. Heart, Hales Corners, 1971, Wi. 53130, USA, pp. 55-56.

43. That which constitutes a miracle in the eyes of Fr. Garrigou-Lagrange (*Christ the Savior*, Saint Louis, 1950, pp. 640 *et seq.*); but other theologians do not share this view.

44. St. Catherine of Siena, *Dialogue*, Paris, 1913, t.I, ch. 78, pp. 270-271: "The Lamb on the Cross was at the same time happy and suffering."

45. P. De Letter, S.J., "Jesus Christ" III, New Catholic Encyclopedia, Washington, 7 (1968), 939.

46. So Catherine Emmerich—(the S.C.D.F. has admitted, by decree of May 16, 1973; ratified on the 18th by Paul VI, the eventual reopening of the cause for beatification)—was said to have been conscious of her baptism at the very moment when, as a newborn babe, she received it; she could write later about this moment: "I saw all my ancestors as far back as the first one who received baptism and a long series of symbolic pictures made me see all the

dangers of the life to come." (R. Auclair, *Prophétie de Catherine Emmerich pour notre temps*, Paris, 1974, pp. 13-14). See also M. Schrader, *"Hildegarde de Bingen* (sainte), "Dict. de Spir., t.7, 1969, col 508 *et seq.*

47. J. Guillet, S.J., *Jésus-Christ dans notre monde*, Paris, 1974, 225 *et seq.* In spite of disagreeing with the author on this point, we appreciate his beautiful pages on other subjects, especially on Christ the doctor (*ibid.*, 62).

48. Cf. E. Bailleu, "La conscience humaine du Christ," *Mélanges de Sc. Rel.* 25 (1968), 29: "time itself, when it is human, finds its ultimate meaning in eternity."

49. It is a common doctrine of the Fathers that the Prophets have predicted what was to be fulfilled centuries later (cf. D.S. 3508) and the Church has always recognized in prophecies very certain signs of the divine origin of the Christian religion, adapted to the intelligence of the men of all times (DS 3539 and especially 3009: Vatican I on the Catholic faith).

50. H. Bars, *Maritain en notre temps*, Paris, 1959, p. 307; J. Maritain, *Court traité de l'existence et de l'existant*, Paris, 1947, pp. 142-145; Saint Thomas, *Sum. Theol.*, Ia, 14, 13c.

51. St. Bonaventure, *Breviloquium IV*, 6; *Opera omnia* (Quarrachi) v. 247 a; cf. L. Iammarrone, art. cité (n. 18), pp. 154-155.

52. Cf. J. Alfaro, art. cité (n. 23), pp. 453ff.; Iammarrone, art. cité (nn. 18-51).

53. J. Alfaro *(op. cit.* [n.23], pp. 455-456) writes: "Christ acquired by the normal way of human apprenticeship the conceptual representations and the very terms with which he translated his filial experience; it suffices to recall the primordial influence that certain images, formulas, Old Testament concepts (for example: the Servant of Yahweh,

the Son of Man, etc.) have exerted on his message. But these same concepts received from the personal experience of Christ a new and transcendental dimension. Moreover this experience could contribute to the formation of concepts and new terms; for example, the invocation 'abba' (Mk. 14:36), with which Christ expressed his intimate experience of divine filiation, was an original creation. More than the formation of new concepts, the personal experience of Christ contributed to the living of the events of his existence in the transcendental light of his filial relation with God and he understood in this same light the words of the Prophets as realized in his Person (Mk. 1:11; 2:28; 8:31; 9:7, 9, 12; 14:62; Lk. 4:18 etc.). The absolute certitude with which Christ utters his doctrine, affirms his divine filiation at the risk of his life and requires from men unconditional adhesion to his Person, this is a reflection of that intimate, metaconceptual light in the field of his conceptual consciousness." The Magisterium of the Church recognizes that the languages used may condition the transmission of Revelation (Declaration Mysterium Ecclesiae, June 24, 1973, AAS 65, 1973, 402).

54. P. De Letter, *op. cit.* (n. 45), p. 939.

55. We are following here in modified terms the article already quoted and praised by L. Iammarrone (note 18), pp. 149, 157-160.

56. F. Bourassa, S.J., "Personne et Conscience en théologie trinitaire," *Gregorianum* 55 (1974), 705-706, n. 45.

57. Fr. Uricchio, OFM, Conv., "Presenza della Chiesa primitiva nel Vangelo di S. Marco," *Misc. Francescana* 66 (1966), 43 and 42; see also p. 47: "The Son of man is Jesus son of God, having become true man." A. Feuillet seems to confirm this

interpretation: Jesus wanted "to express his unique relation with God as Son and as the agent of salvation" *(loc. cit.,* n. 8, p. 539, n. 2).

58. Th. Preiss, *Le Fils de l'Homme, Etudes Théologiques et Religieuses,* 26 (1951) 3, 76.

59. As a well known exegete has written, "the gospel facts oblige one to admit in Jesus a knowledge from above and a knowledge from below which is essentially progressive and experiential. But an attentive reading of the gospel texts obliges one to distinguish, in the science from above, a knowledge of vision (beatific vision) and an infused knowledge. (August 22, 1976).—On the various doctrinal qualifications of various aspects of the doctrine of the Church on the triple human knowledge of Jesus, one can consult the excellent presentation of Xiberta *(op. cit.* n. 1), pp. 405-406. In order to resume and complete this I shall say that it is at least "proximum fidei" that one must exclude from the soul of Christ from the first moment of its creation all ignorance; and from the moment it enjoys the beatific vision; it is of faith that Jesus enjoyed at least at certain moments of his earthly life the infused knowledge of the Prophet; it is implicitly revealed that Jesus exercised an experimental and acquired knowledge. Moreover the historian can affirm with moral certitude (not absolute) proper to his discipline, that Jesus claimed the knowledge of vision of his Father and a knowledge of a Prophet.

60. Encycl. *Pascendi* (DS 3494-3497): the modernists wanted to attribute to the faith and not to history all that surpassed the natural condition of man in Christ, all that went beyond His psychological condition in regard to His place and His time; whence the tendency to reduce the saying of Christ to that which did not seem to exceed the capacity of His audience. Analogous tendencies are at work today.

61. Cf. L. Malevez, *op. cit.* (n. 9), p. 131.

62. *Mystici Corporis*, 1943, pp. 215-219; cf. *Sum. Theol.*, IIIa, 11:1; 7:1.

63. Galtier, *op. cit.*, §334, p. 263; Maritian, *De la grâce et de l'humanité de Jésus*, p. 122.

64. Vogtle, *op. cit.*, p. 99.

65. Pastoral letter of the bishops of Belgium on "*notre foi en Jésus-Christ*," §17, *Nouv. Rev. Théol.*, 90 (1968), 18.

66. *Mystici Corporis*, a text quoted in part by DS 3812; it needs to be completed: "In praesepibus, in cruce, in sempiterna Patris gloria omnia Ecclesiae membra Christus sibi conspecta sibique conjuncta habet longe clarius, longeque amantius, quam mater filium suum in gremio positum quam quilibet semetipsum cognoscit ac diliget" (AAS 35, 1943, 230; cf. 215). Therefore, on the cross Jesus enjoyed the beatific vision, in which He saw us. Many moderns, following Luther (cf. M. Lienhard, *Luther, témoin de Jésus-Christ*, Paris, 1973, 120 *et seq.)* no longer accept this doctrinal view; what is less well known, however, is that Luther taught that Christ knew the day of judgment, as man, even before His resurrection (cf. A. Vacant, DTC 1, col. 589).

67. I remember having asked a famous American Methodist theologian if he was of the opinion that St. Paul was thinking here of Christ as God or as man; he answered that he had never reflected on this subject.... Many others live no doubt in an unconscious monophysism and, contenting themselves with believing in the divine love of Christ for them, do not even ask themselves if the Crucified Christ loved them individually with a human love. Such is not the case of C. Duquoc however: "Christ saves men by entering into their condition. It does not belong to the human condition to keep up a par-

ticular relationship with each face. Whatever the
eschatological plan, there is no question of denying
it. Christ reaches this concrete universality by the
Resurrection. It is in obscurity that Jesus worked
out the salvation of the world. The universal love of
Christ does not require universal knowledge."

(*Christologie*, Paris, 1968, t.I, p. 166). We refer
back to note 35 and to the explanation given there,
according to St. Robert Bellarmine, of the entry of
Christ into our human condition, together with its
consequences. Duquoc seems to disregard here the
concrete character of the redemptive work of Christ.
How could He have expiated as man, as the new
Adam, the sins which He had not known as man?
Moreover, the Magisterium has made a pronounce-
ment to this effect (cf. note 66). To return to Pauline
terms, let us say that it is in obedience as a man, in
the form of a slave, that the Son of God saved the
world. Paul, who had not known Christ according to
the flesh, was nevertheless sure that Jesus had
"delivered himself up for him" (Ga. 2:20) and he did
not exclude the will of the human form from His
oblation, which could not be the work of the divinity
as such, purely and simply without consideration of
the humanity.

68. Cf. N. Spaccapelo, S.J., "La coscienza di
Cristo," *Science et Esprit* 26 (1974), 33. A study
that is remarkably clear, in the light of B. Lonergan.

69. What we mean by this term is made explicit
in the following paragraphs. Read in D.T.C., I, col
595-596, the conclusion of the article by A. Vacant
on the *"Agnoètes."* Their error, anathematized by
Leporius along with the bishops of Gaul and Africa,
by St. Gregory the Great, Eulogius, St. Sophrone in
a letter read at the Sixth Ecumenical Council (680)
was rejected unanimously by the ordinary and

universal Magisterium of the Church. One can and must say, returning in the contemporary context to what Pétau said with regard to the Agnoetae, that the error of the Neo-Agnoetae is an error close to heresy (D.T.C., *ibid.*).

70. C. de Foucauld, *Contemplation,* Paris ç970: "In loving me and looking at me in all the moments of my life from all the moments of yours, you oblige me to say to you that I love you in all the moments of my life" (p. 84). "As man...He rejoiced at every moment of His life in the faithfulness of our love and suffered because of our infidelities" (p. 86). "My God, make me console you as much as possible during all the instants of my life" (p. 87).

71. Pius XI, *Miserentissimus Redemptor,* AAS 20 (1928), 173 *et seq.*

72. Cf. A. Koller, *op. cit.*, no. 42, p. 124; Pius XI, *Mis. Redemptor, op. cit.,* p. 178.

73. B. de Margerie, *Le Christ pour le Monde,* Paris, 1971, p. 232, n. 7.

74. Cf. St. Thomas, *Sum. Theol.,* III a 9, a c: "that which is in potency cannot be reduced to act except by what is already in act: thus it is necessary that a body be warm in order to warm other bodies. But man is in potency to the knowledge of the blessed which consists of the vision of God, ordered to it as his end. Men are led to this end by the humanity of Christ: Hb. 2:10. The vision of God was supremely fitting to Christ as man, since the cause is always more perfect than the effect. The humanity of Christ cannot be the mediator of the beatific vision if it does not possess it.

75. Following St. Augustine, St. Fulgentius of Ruspe, in his XIVth letter to Ferrand, gathered the biblical texts which present the human knowledge of Jesus: ML 65, 416ff., and Thomassin (*Dogmata Theologica,* Vivès, Paris, 1868, t. IV, *De Incarna-*

tione VII, 1 pp. 1-4) comments notably on this letter, which had such a great influence on later theology.

76. Cf. St. Thomas Aquinas, *Compendium Theologiae*, I, 232. Under the influence of St. Augustine, St. Thomas recognizes that in every man, including Christ, there exists a superior reason to contemplate eternity and a lower reason which considers temporal realities.

77. "Amantissima cognitio," says Pius XII *(Mystici Corporis,* D.S. 3812).

78. Thomassin *(op. cit.,* n. 78, t. IV, VII, 7, 11, p. 41) writes: "Incarnatio Verbi hominis assumpti beatificatio" and gives many reasons: "Beatitudo ipsa Deus est. Ergo, cum infunditur humanitati Deus, infunditur illi beatitudo.... Ecqua autem beatitudo, quae se non intelligit?" One may question whether Thomassin is applying well the rules of the "communication of idioms." His text is in any case clearly opposed to "the immediate non-beatifying vision" proclaimed by K. Rahner. This theory seems to disregard completely the fact that the divine Essence, seen face to face, is Beatitude.

79. Rahner, who leaves aside the infused knowledge, affirms the immediate (non-beatifying) vision, while Duquoc adopts the opposite position (cf. texts quoted in notes 6, 7 and 24). By adding up the affirmations of the Neo-Agnoetae authors one would obtain approximately the statements of Church doctrine. But the temptation of many of their readers is to add up their negations and errors.... In any case, it would be interesting and useful to show how they refute each other to a certain extent.

80. We shall mention here two points which need to be studied further. The first relates to the agreement between infused knowledge and acquired knowledge. If the former is already conceptual, in what sense does it need the latter? The

reader should compare notes 38, 53, 62 and 63. Without forgetting that human language has, in the last analysis, its own origin in God the Creator. Without forgetting either that in the simplicity of His divine essence (the origin of this language) God knows our complex statements. (St. Thomas, *Sum. Theol.*, Ia, 14, 14; *Summa contra Gentiles* I, 57, 58). Nothing therefore prevents the Word from having communicated to His humanity as Mediator an infused knowledge of our human concepts, also received subsequently by His education. The second concerns import and significance of "I" in St. John (cf. notes 20 and 21). Does it not mean first of all the eternal Person of the Word, then, secondarily, in the instrumental sense, the action that this Person exercises through the instrument of His human liberty? Is this not the usual meaning of "I" in St. John's Gospel, on the lips of Jesus?

Daughters of St. Paul

IN MASSACHUSETTS
  50 St. Paul's Ave. Jamaica Plain, Boston, MA 02130;
    617-522-8911; 617-522-0875;
  172 Tremont Street, Boston, MA 02111; **617-426-5464;**
    617-426-4230
IN NEW YORK
  78 Fort Place, Staten Island, NY 10301; **212-447-5071**
  59 East 43rd Street, New York, NY 10017; **212-986-7580**
  7 State Street, New York, NY 10004; **212-447-5071**
  625 East 187th Street, Bronx, NY 10458; **212-584-0440**
  525 Main Street, Buffalo, NY 14203; **716-847-6044**
IN NEW JERSEY
  Hudson Mall — Route 440 and Communipaw Ave.,
    Jersey City, NJ 07304; **201-433-7740**
IN CONNECTICUT
  202 Fairfield Ave., Bridgeport, CT 06604; **203-335-9913**
IN OHIO
  2105 Ontario St. (at Prospect Ave.), Cleveland, OH 44115; **216-621-9427**
  25 E. Eighth Street, Cincinnati, OH 45202; **513-721-4838**
IN PENNSYLVANIA
  1719 Chestnut Street, Philadelphia, PA 19103; **215-568-2638**
IN FLORIDA
  2700 Biscayne Blvd., Miami, FL 33137; **305-573-1618**
IN LOUISIANA
  4403 Veterans Memorial Blvd., Metairie, LA 70002; **504-887-7631;**
    504-887-0113
  1800 South Acadian Thruway, P.O. Box 2028, Baton Rouge, LA 70821
    504-343-4057; 504-343-3814
IN MISSOURI
  1001 Pine Street (at North 10th), St. Louis, MO 63101; **314-621-0346;**
    314-231-1034
IN ILLINOIS
  172 North Michigan Ave., Chicago, IL 60601; **312-346-4228**
IN TEXAS
  114 Main Plaza, San Antonio, TX 78205; **512-224-8101**
IN CALIFORNIA
  1570 Fifth Avenue, San Diego, CA 92101; **714-232-1442**
  46 Geary Street, San Francisco, CA 94108; **415-781-5180**
IN HAWAII
  1143 Bishop Street, Honolulu, HI 96813; **808-521-2731**
IN ALASKA
  750 West 5th Avenue, Anchorage AK 99501; **907-272-8183**
IN CANADA
  3022 Dufferin Street, Toronto 395, Ontario, Canada
IN ENGLAND
  128, Notting Hill Gate, London W11 3QG, England
133 Corporation Street, Birmingham B4 6PH, England
5A-7 Royal Exchange Square, Glasgow G1 3AH, England
82 Bold Street, Liverpool L1 4HR, England
IN AUSTRALIA
  58 Abbotsford Rd., Homebush, N.S.W., Sydney 2140, Australia